Needlework

From Domestic Oppression
                to Artistic Expression

Tilly Du Buisson

Introduction

The practice of needlework has historically been used to perpetuate the oppression of women, but in recent years feminist artists have increasingly returned to the medium. This essay looks at these artists and investigates whether it is possible to reclaim a historically oppressive practice within a feminist project for emancipation. Does this return to needlework perpetuate or transform oppressive gender norms? And in what ways is it possible for women to reclaim needlework?

  The act of sewing may appear simple, even mundane but it carries the weight of centuries of domesticity, gender roles and expectations. It evokes an image of a woman in a long gown, hunched over by a window, her fingers working to guide the needle through fabric. But the stitch is more than a connection between fabric and thread: it links the past with the present, transforms oppression into reclamation and creates community for the isolated.

  Like many others, I grew up surrounded by, amongst many other pastimes, the knitting and sewing projects of both my Grannies. I would sit in awe of my Great Grandmother's intricate embroidery of Drum Castle in Banchory, Scotland. About a metre long, it hung proudly in the sitting room. I would sit up close and admire the stitches, each one representing a part of my Scottish heritage. Over time a lot of my own art projects introduced more and more textile artists, the likes of Anni Albers and Louise Bourgeois. I couldn't stay away from them. I began to find myself so drawn to needlework. What was it about it that resonated so strongly with me? My curiosity grew into a need to delve deep into the craft to understand the layers of history and legacy embedded within it.

In the introduction of *The Second Sex*, Simone de Beauvoir writes: "But if I wish to define myself, I must first of all say: 'I am a woman'". Beauvoir recognises that within society women are seen as the 'other' gender. Men are not defined by their genders whereas a woman is always reduced to hers. Women have to do this because they are not the 'neutral' gender. Beauvoir also points out the biological differences between men and women writing about the long history of women's constraint within prejudiced ideas about their reproductive system. She recognises that women are confined by society's perception of their bodies: 'she thinks with her glands'. Men can overlook their hormonal function and their bodies are 'a direct and normal connection with the world' rather than something hindering them. Beauvoir acknowledges society's ingrained bias where the masculine is valued more highly than the feminine.

She expands on that by acknowledging that the reduction of women to their gender has resulted in their sexual objectification. Men struggle to perceive women as anything 'other' than sex; a woman is no more than what she offers biologically. This one-dimensional perspective on women has created a limited understanding of women's emotions and intelligence within patriarchal society. A limited understanding of women's intellectual and creative capability leads to the undervaluation of certain practices associated with femininity and domesticity; society cannot appreciate and understand the depth of practices like needlework.

Given the deep-rooted sexism throughout history, especially Black, lower-class and Queer women, the need to reassert certain aspects of their femininity becomes not just clear but urgent. Reclamation under feminism is the conscious and deliberate attempt to reassert and repurpose elements that have historically been weaponised against women. It's about acknowledging the history of marginalisation and turning that around by subverting stereotypes, turning that around and subverting stereotypes, occupying spaces women were once denied access to. The reclamation of words like 'bitch' is an example of feminists taking back what's theirs. Songs like Doja Cat's 'Boss Bitch' have transformed a slur once used to belittle women and turned it around to represent strength.

Many feminists would argue that 'bitch' can't be used in an empowering way, that it reinforces the sexism that it aims to subvert. The debate around reclaiming terms and practices that have historically been used to oppress women remains a constant conversation within feminist discourse; a constant question of what can be truly reclaimed and what, perhaps, should be left behind.

To begin to understand the complexities of needlework's journey of being such an undervalued practice, we firstly have to think about the historical development of needlework and how it came to be seen as a 'domestic' and 'feminine' practice. Understanding the oppressive past of needlework, the ways it has kept women at home and the ways it forces women today to work in harsh conditions for little to no money brings me to question whether or not we can reclaim needlework under feminism. Can we reclaim an act once used to oppress women and transform it into a feminist tool? By attempting to reclaim a suppressive act of the past are we perpetuating harmful stereotypes or are we transforming them?

The importance of needlework in feminist conversations is undeniable, especially with a surge in women-led exhibitions such as the Barbican's *Unraveled: The Power and Politics of Textiles in Art*. During COVID-19, we saw a rise in crafts like crocheting and knitting, with one Forbes headline proclaiming 'Knitting Has Become The Cool Activity During The Coronavirus Crisis'.

As exhibitions gain prominence and more people pick up these crafts, it's essential to both celebrate the reclamation of needlework and acknowledge its historical context. As we learn more about the intersection of needlework and feminism we need to bring up and discuss the contradictions within major galleries like the Barbican, which support feminist narratives on one hand but continue to align with institutions or countries whose policies can undermine feminist values. This tension calls for critical examination of how feminist exhibitions can challenge broader institutional affiliations and policies that contradict their messages of empowerment.

Additionally we also need to confront needlework's complex place within the fast fashion industry, where garment labour continues to economically and physically oppress many women in developing countries. How can these exhibitions bring attention to both the empowering aspects of needlework as an art form and the exploitation that remains deeply embedded in the fashion industry? By initiating these discussions, we create an opportunity for greater awareness and empowerment. What narratives should be prioritised, and how can we keep these conversations going to drive real change?

By examining feminist theorist Judith Butler's concept of gender performativity, we gain a more nuanced understanding of the social construction of gender norms, helping us learn how to transform them. We can then start to understand whether embracing and transforming traditionally 'feminine' practices such as needlework can align with feminist ideas. One might assume that by engaging in practices like needlework, that have a complex history for women, we are perpetuating existing essentialist gender stereotypes. Yet, as Amelia Jones argues in her essay *Essentialism, Feminism and Art: Spaces Where Woman "Oozes away,"* we need a more complex understanding of essentialism within feminist art. By practising needlework it may appear that we are perpetuating existing gendered structures but in order to transform them we must first acknowledge them. Drawing on the conceptual framework afforded by these feminist thinkers, as well as the rebellious and brave works of Tracey Emin, Louise Bourgeois and the women of the Chilean Arpilleras workshops, in what follows I aim to demonstrate the role of needlework in building resistance, resilience and connection.

Tilly Du Buisson

Fundamentals of Needlework

In 2018, I visited a major retrospective of textile artist Anni Albers's work that took place at the Tate Modern, a turning point for the representation of women's work within the prestigious art world. Exhibitions featuring solely female artists have been scarce in the past: Marina Abramovic's recent show at the Royal Academy of Art was the first ever female retrospective there. Whilst female artists continue to be highly underrepresented, we are beginning to see a shift in this representation as more major art galleries are showcasing female artists. Women's needlework in particular has faced greater underrepresentation within the arts where for such a long time it hasn't been perceived as 'proper' art.

Albers studied at the Bauhaus, a school famous for its radical approach to art and design post World War I. Despite the radical approaches happening within the school, women were largely discouraged from the fine arts and relegated to the crafts. Albers found herself pushed towards weaving, a practice often perceived as simply decorative. However, that didn't stop her from challenging these ideas, instead showing weaving to be a practice of great self expression. Albers's refusal to be confined wasn't loud or defiant; it was steady, deliberate, and innovative. Through her exploration of unconventional materials, bold modernist patterns, and Constructivist influences, she quietly but powerfully redefined weaving as a boundary-pushing art form.

Despite what you might think about needlework having always been associated with the female gender and femininity, it hasn't always been this way. When I began to dig deeper into the history of needlework I discovered how both men and women have practised needlework, men all around the world took part in the textile industry. In ancient Egypt, men participated in every stage of textile production, from harvesting fibres to weaving, while in medieval Europe, men dominated needlework when it held economic value leaving women to unpaid domestic needlework as men took the wages. Societal expectations confined women to responsibility, only allowing them to practise needlework in the home. This is when the gender difference becomes clear: men's work was paid whereas women's was for the purpose of survival and decoration. Men took away the economic value of needlework from women.

Men controlled the commercial textile industry, upholding the patriarchal standards of the time and further taking economic and social power away from women. So, if men were predominantly controlling the textile industry, it prompts us to wonder, when did needlework actually become closely associated with women?

The expectation that women should stay at home and practise needlework exclusively within the home was for women of all classes. However, during the Middle Ages, not all women had the same rights and privileges due to differences in social status and class.

Lisa Vinebaum notes in *Unsettling Women's Work* that it was a privilege for women to exclusively stay in the home. Those women who did have to practise paid needlework faced harsher pay and conditions than before men took over and women's wages would go to their fathers/husbands. She further points out that the prevailing 'understandings of "women's work" have been defined through Eurocentric, classed, and white-privileged perspectives while being presented as universal experiences'. History tends to overlook the experiences of the less privileged and in this case the middle and upper-class image of women staying at home dominates, creating the idea that needlework was predominantly domestic.

In the 16th century, these patriarchal standards persisted and women were to obey the wishes of their husbands. Rosika Parker writes about how sexual difference relates to needlework, discussing how women were discouraged from partaking in 'activities associated with masculinity' and instead should practise activities with a 'gentle delicacy'. Religious influence continued to lead the way for what gender roles were and women were taught that they must stay at home, cook and have children, which made needlework the perfect practice to go alongside those domestic duties. She continues: 'embroidery was extolled as the quintessential occupation for women' because it was presumed that woman's strength wasn't suited for strenuous tasks. Needlework started to be thought of as a strictly 'simple' and less 'intellectual' practice because of the fact that it could be performed in the home, amongst other duties. The domestic connotations around needlework dominated society, ultimately leading to its feminisation, despite men having practised needlework too.

The combination of women being granted a lower socio-economic status on the one hand, and the association between women and needlework on the other, ultimately led to a separation of needlework from the fine arts. Society's view of femininity enabled needlework to be considered a lesser practice. As Griselda Pollock discusses in *Old mistresses: Women, Art and Ideology*, needlework lay far below painting and sculpture within the hierarchy of the arts; it was considered a decorative art. Pollock and Parker make it clear that needlework was considered a less intellectual and strenuous practice because of the domestic sphere it was practised in. Fine art was public, often made in art schools or art studios for galleries or markets and was made to be sold, made to be seen. Women's needlework was confined to the home and their work was never seen; it was for love and comfort. Women were making textiles like clothes for their children and curtains for the home, the nature of their work perceived as a necessity which contributed ultimately to the undervaluation of the practice.

Upper middle-class women could assert and nurture their femininity by creating a comfortable home with well-clothed family members. By learning to make delicate and intricate pieces they could demonstrate how devoted they were to their families and home. Many lower-class families, however, couldn't afford for their women not to work. For lower-class women, needlework was a practice of survival. They had to work tirelessly for little money, practising needlework to financially support their families. Though different for each, the purpose of needlework for each class of women demonstrates how the practice has been consistently undervalued in society

Needlework is just one of the many practices that is undervalued due to its association with femininity and domesticity. In many professions today, women still face discrimination because of the previous associations their practice has with the home. In cooking, men massively occupy the industry with only 20% of head chefs being women. Women are arguably less respected and less likely to be hired, perhaps partly because of the typical domestic connotations of cooking, that is, the idea that women can only cook for the home, for love, for comfort. This discrimination of women in the culinary industry is similar to needlework within the arts. It is only today that we are beginning to see exhibitions celebrating needlework artists like Anni Albers in galleries like the Tate Modern and we are beginning to see a shift in the way women's work is being recognised.

By the 17th century some middle and upper-class women were able to gain a basic education through embroidery samplers. The education they received, however, still reinforced traditional gender roles. In *The Subversive Stitch*, Parker highlights that the emphasis of this education wasn't on the intellectual development of the women but rather on the development of their sewing skills for their futures as homemakers. There were different levels to signify how developed a woman's embroidery skills were, starting off with basic patterns moving on to more tricky alphabets. These levels taught women at such a young age that their embroidery skills were more important than their education. Although their educational efforts were channelled into domestic labours, it is still important to recognise the importance of this education; most women at the time, especially lower-class women, were denied the opportunity to be educated. This introduction to basic education, like learning the alphabet through embroidery, still had great significance as it gave many women the opportunity to subvert the stitch.

The 17th century was a turning point in which women across the world started using needlework as a form of resistance and resilience. In Lisa Vinebaum's *Unsettling Women's Work*, she writes about how European colonists took control over indigenous materials, textile systems and trade routes to set up a capitalist system. Colonists enslaved millions of African women to make textiles for no money in extremely harsh conditions. They were given next to no clothing and their living conditions were cold; they had to come up with solutions using what was around them. Women started collecting scraps from their factories and layering them, creating thick quilts to keep themselves and their families warm. These quilts were also an outlet for artistic and self-expression, allowing them to find community, tell stories and gain financial independence.

The artistry of Harriet Powers is a testament to this. Her 'Pictorial Quilt', crafted in 1895, tells biblical stories through the lens of her experience as an African American slave. Powers's quilt not only captures her spirituality and personal narrative but also stands as a symbol of resilience, setting the tone for how women have reclaimed this practice. Through needlework, generations of women redefined a form imposed upon

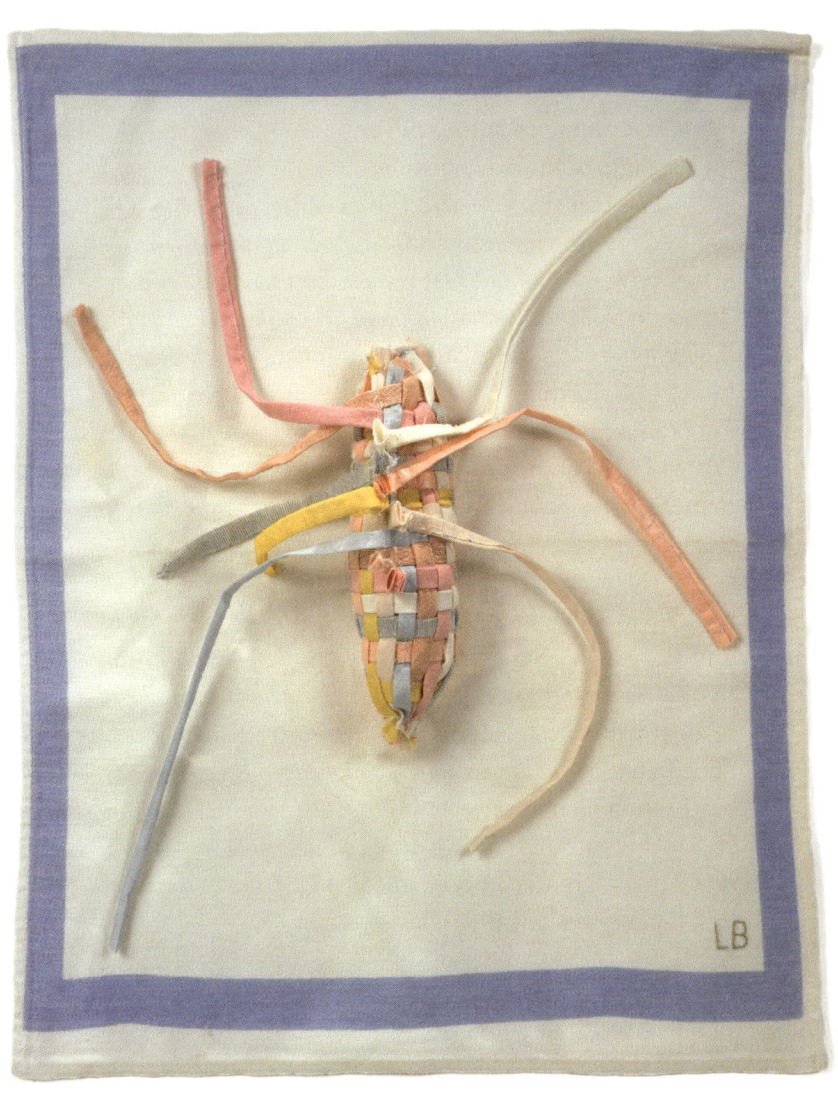

SPIDER, Louise Bourgeois, 2007

Fabric and fabric collage; 41.6 x 33.7 x 6.4 cm
Photo: Christopher Burke
The Easton Foundation / Licensed by DACS, London

them, layering each stitch with endurance, meaning and the strength of their own hands.

The British Women's Suffrage Movement, which secured the vote for women, is another significant example of how throughout history women have used their domestic skills to their advantage. Those involved in the movement made feminist banners for their demonstrations, transforming the skills that taught them to stay at home and be quiet into a tool of empowerment. The 'Votes for Women, Huddersfield' banner from 1910 demonstrates how women powerfully used the stitch to protest and assert female strength.

The everyday practice of needlework has been so belittled in society but by looking at both Harriet Powers and the work of the suffragettes, we can just begin to see how needlework holds importance in the fight against prejudice. Needlework has been the only real acceptable outlet for women's creativity and it is worth celebrating instances where that hasn't limited women. By looking into the basic history of needlework we can now have a greater appreciation for the specific works that I go on to analyse.

Tilly Du Buisson

Gender and Needlework

In *Gender Trouble* by Judith Butler they argue that gender roles are constructs not something innate; we are not born with an essentially 'masculine' or 'feminine' way of being or set of behaviours. Instead, they argue that gender is 'performed'. Butler is suggesting that, without knowing, humanity conforms to societal norms and expectations associated with our assigned gender. Butler says: 'Gender is the repeated stylization of the body, a set of repeated acts within a highly rigid regulatory frame that congeal over time to produce the appearance of substance, of a natural sort of being'. These specific gendered behaviours that we perform can take various forms: bodily movement, appearance, jobs, hobbies and language. Butler's recognition of gender being performative calls for a more complex understanding, acknowledging that gender is fluid rather than fixed: 'When the constructed status of gender is theorised as radically independent of sex, gender itself becomes a free floating artiface'. This statement implies that if we can, as a society, begin to understand how gender is socially constructed, we can step outside of conventional ideas that gender norms follow 'naturally' and 'essentially' from biological sex. Once we accept that gender isn't innate, but a set of social norms, this illuminates how we look at the women who have challenged these norms with traditional 'feminine' practices such as needlework. I turn to the art of Tracey Emin and Louise Bourgeois to explore and question the ways in which female artists have transformed needlework as a practice.

'The reluctant hero of feminist art' Louise Bourgeois, confidently welcomed femininity into her practice through her use of needlework, exploring soft sculptures and weaving. Bourgeois was bold and unafraid in her approach to various topics around womanhood, like motherhood, sexuality and the female body, her work challenging gender roles and patriarchy. In Bourgeois's piece 'untitled' from 2008 a woven spider is stitched onto a piece of fabric. Bourgeois has a preoccupation with spiders throughout her work, using them as a symbol of feminine power. Bourgeois dedicated the spiders in her work to her mother, saying: 'Like a spider, my mother was a weaver ... Like spiders, my mother was very clever'. Bourgeois's choice of language in this comparison between the spider and her mother challenges patriarchal ideas that women are weak and unintelligent.

The idea of embracing femininity within feminism has been debated extensively throughout feminist discourse over time, particularly during second wave feminism. There was an opposing view amongst many feminists that in order to dismantle patriarchy, women needed to reject traditionally 'feminine' roles and behaviours. Feminist Catherine MacKinnon says: 'femininity is defined and enforced by men, and women are forced through ideological indoctrination to embody femininity as the sexually submissive complement to masculine sexual dominance and power'. 'Ideological indoctrination' refers to the process through which individuals or groups are taught to accept a particular set of beliefs or ideologies without questioning them. MacKinnon suggests that femininity is a one-dimensional characteristic, suggesting that a woman who is feminine is submissive and that if she desires to escape masculine dominance, she has to reject femininity. As Betty Luther Hilman writes in her essay *The Clothes I Wear Help Me To Know My Own Power: The Politics of Gender Presentation in the Era of Women's Liberation'*, women rejected femininity through rejecting traditional beauty standards. One example she gives is women shaving their hair, saying that 'cutting one's hair was thus a symbolic escape from patriarchal standards of feminine beauty' and 'short hair is a symbol of emancipation'. By shaving their heads, these women not only freed themselves from the time consuming, costly maintenance of long hair but also made some way towards freeing themselves from objectification by men and from traditional, oppressive feminine beauty standards. Many second wave feminists believed that through the rejection of femininity they could find freedom. This then leads us back to Bourgeois's use of needlework: is she perpetuating harmful stereotypes about women by practising such a traditionally 'feminine' practice? And to what extent is her work feminist?

One might assume Bourgeois's use of the form reiterates the aforementioned 'essentialist' ideas about gender, discussed by art theorist Amelia Jones. When discussing essentialism in feminist art, Jones examines

Judy Chicago and the discourse surrounding her work. A lot of Chicago's work centres on the vagina, saying that it represents 'the stamp of femaleness'. She aims to challenge previous negative ideas of the female body and vagina, celebrating them instead. Jones highlights in the essay how many feminist art historians have disagreed with Chicago's centring of the vagina, writing that: 'Feminist theorists reacted strongly against what they perceived either as a brute essentialism [...] or as a less direct but equally insidious courting of essentialism through repeating stereotypes associated with femininity or females'.

Though Jones acknowledges this argument from some feminists about Chicago's work, for her the idea is more complex. She makes the argument that within feminism there will always be a certain degree of essentialism because of the deep-rooted essentialism within politics, culture and theory. The discussion of femininity and the female body within society makes it hard for feminist artists to completely remove essentialist traits from their art. Jones writes: 'Any method that seeks to analyse existing modes of identification, address modes of oppression of particular groups or classes of identified subjects, and open ways for change will entail essentializing moments'. She recognises that in order to address oppression there will be moments of apparent essentialism. Jones recognises that in order to challenge existing structures, stereotypes and norms, it is necessary to acknowledge the aspects that need transformation. As we attempt to challenge and transform oppression, it may sometimes involve an approach where one appears to be perpetuating harmful stereotypes.

However, as Jones argues, within feminist art, this is often a strategic process aiming to represent how gender norms can be subverted. To effectively convey one's message, an artist may need to openly reflect on and sometimes imitate past oppressive behaviours. Rather than completely ignoring harmful stereotypes and essentialist frameworks, as many second wave feminists did, it may be important to some feminists that they acknowledge their unique experiences of these frameworks to encourage a deeper understanding of gender.

Jones's understanding allows us to look at Bourgeois's work and understand how her employment of needlework is not perpetuating harmful stereotypes around the practice and women but transforming them. Bourgeois uses needlework to represent traditional femininity but, upon closer investigation, she is using the form to strategically challenge gender norms.

Bourgeois had already established a successful career in painting and sculpture by the time she started to focus on needlework, which furthers the idea that Bourgeois's choice to use needlework was strategic. She acknowledges the practice's historical association with domesticity and femininity, saying: 'When I was growing up, all the women in my house were using needles. I've always had a fascination with the needle, the magic power of the needle'. She acknowledges the potential of the needle and explores it in her own powerful way.

I first discovered the work of Bourgeois in 2021 when I visited her exhibition *The Woven Child* at the Hayward Gallery. I was completely moved by her works

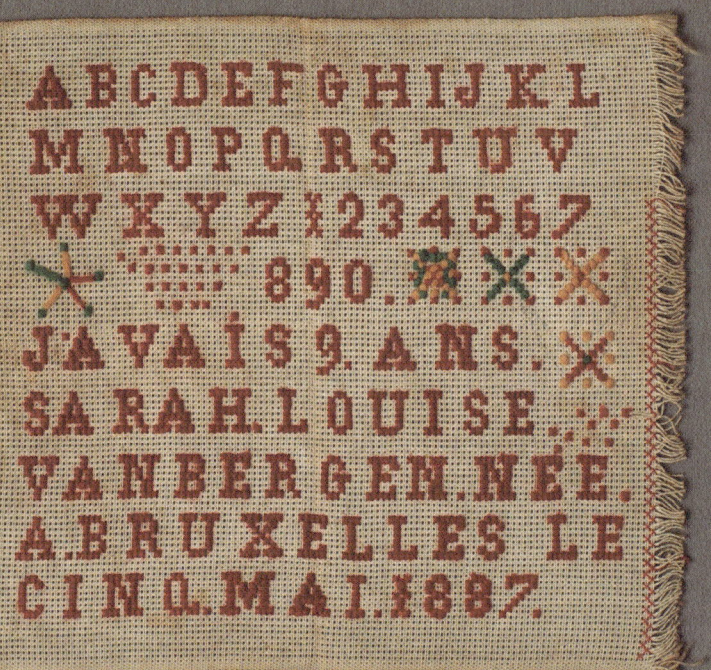

SAMPLER, Sarah Louise Vanbergen, 1896
Collection MoMu Antwerp, inv. T98/171
Photo: Daniel Rys

and this was the first and only exhibition where I've cried. I immediately planned my next visit for the following week with another friend and proceeded to go another time after that. Her works have such a delicate feel to them yet they prompt such bold feelings of anger and woe. She embodies the complex feelings and beauty of womanhood. Bourgeois evokes in us a desire to question the female experience. I imagine feminist art would be in such a different place if Bourgeois was dismissed from it, simply because of the use of femininity in her work.

Expanding on Jones's perspective, Tracey Emin's work emerges as a significant example of strategic essentialism's subversive potential. Like Bourgeois, Emin embraces and reinterprets traditionally feminine themes, transforming them into bold statements on identity and gender. By engaging with feminine symbols she doesn't just replicate established norms but weaponises them, mirroring Judith Butler's theory of drag as a technique for dismantling gender roles. As we will see, Emin's engagement in mimicry transforms conventional understandings of feminine practices and the 'feminine' as such, much like drag artists.

Emin challenges gender norms and demonstrates the fluidity of gender in many of her pieces. She has produced a range of provocative pieces, her work tending to revolve around love, vulnerability, sex and identity. I'm particularly interested in Emin's use of needlework in her appliqued quilts, specifically 'Psyco Slut' where Emin uses needlework to layer patches of fabric. The piece subverts gender norms through Emin's combination of traditional 'masculine' and 'feminine' traits: patches of pinks, pastels and florals to epitomise femininity and vulgar language to represent the 'masculine'. By looking at the ways in which society has taught women how to use language, a semantics of gender is revealed. In his study of language used by different genders, Lakoff suggests that women's use of language perpetuates a stereotype of weakness, 'Lakoff argues that swear words do not fit in the frame of speech for women, by using this language they can appear rough and aggressive', whereas if a man uses swear words he may be considered powerful and strong. Lakoff suggests that women using vulgar language can be seen as a threat to men's power within society. Emin breaks expectations that are placed on her due to her perceived gender by using words like 'slut' and 'shit' in her piece. She also challenges the typical understanding of femininity by publicly talking about her emotions and sex, which women have been shamed for in the past. This piece feels rebellious and witty because of Emin's conscious use of vulgar language under the disguise of the 'feminine' practice of needlework.

I revisit *Gender Trouble* to draw comparisons between Emin's 'Psyco Slut' and Butler's inquiry into the performance of drag. Drag is the exaggerated performance of either femininity or masculinity by the opposing gender and, consequently, drag helps us to understand gender performativity. Butler says that: 'in imitating gender, drag implicitly reveals the imitative structure of gender itself — as well as its contingency'. Butler talks about drag to demonstrate their theory that gender is performed and to argue that drag, by playfully exposing the 'constructedness' of gender itself, subverts existing gender norms. Butler argues that drag illustrates how gender roles are learned and therefore changeable and so it creates an openness for re-interpretation around gender. This is because drag artists do not directly imitate femininity or masculinity but exaggerate it, reclaiming and subverting gender stereotypes. To highlight the false nature of gender, transforming it into comedic expressions. In both drag and Emin's work with needlework, gender takes a new form. Emin reclaims needlework as her own, liberating it from its oppressive past. Emin doesn't just reclaim the needle, she also reclaims sexist language with the use of the derogatory word 'slut' as her own.

Emin has achieved exactly what she set out for. She has disturbed many with her artwork by asking them to confront subjects of sexuality and femininity. The right-wing tabloid Daily Mail has extensively criticised Emin labelling her work as 'embarrassing' and 'infuriating'. It's unsurprising that a tabloid aligned with right-wing ideology would find Emin's work thus, as it directly challenges conventional gender norms which right-wing ideology tends to perpetuate and cling to. Her work causes people who align with such ideologies to become uncomfortable, dismissing her work as nonsensical and trivial.

With the help of theorists such as Jones and Butler we can understand better how needlework can be reclaimed within feminist art. Artists such as Bourgeois and Emin both combine and subvert gender roles to reimagine gender as a spectrum, allowing us to see how femininity can be expressed in many ways.

Theorist Simone De Beauvoir says 'I recall also

a young Trotskyite standing on a platform at a boisterous meeting and getting ready to use her fists, in spite of her evident fragility. She was denying her feminine weakness'. De Beauvoir points out how women deny their own feminine traits in certain situations to appear stronger, demonstrating how society teaches us that it is only through masculinity that we can be powerful. She uses this example of the women on the platform to illustrate societal perceptions of men as superior. This quote from De Beauvoir further illuminates how gender is performed and, therefore, how practices like needlework can be used to reimagine femininity.

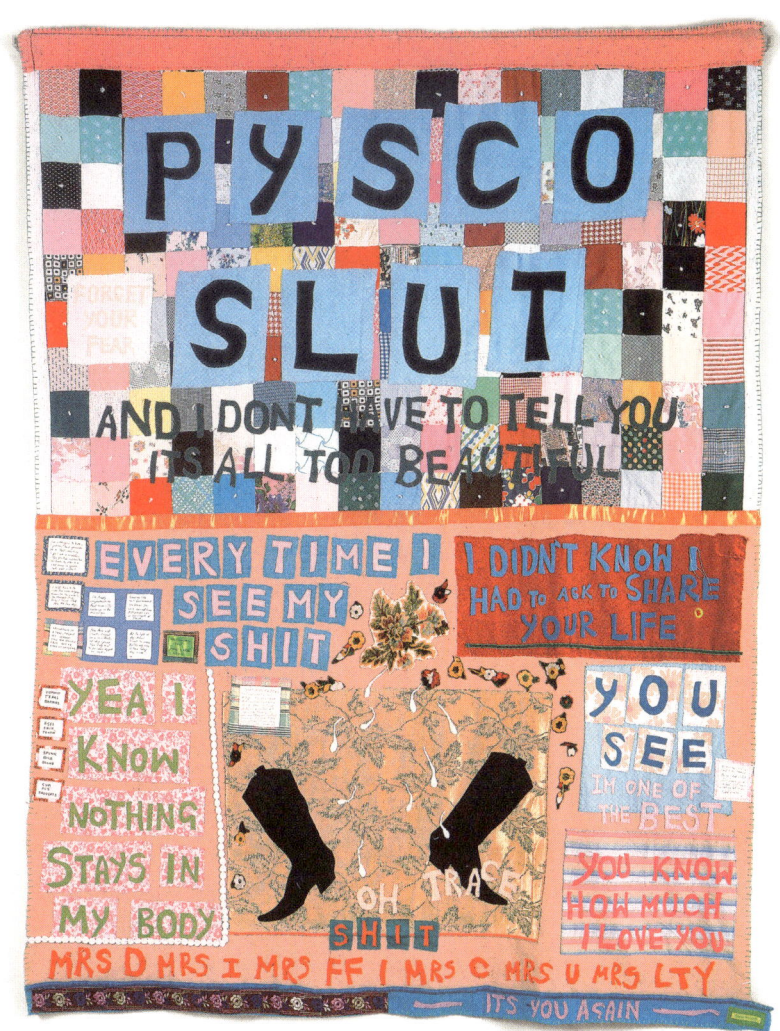

PYSCO SLUT, Tracey Emin, 1999

Tracey Emin. All rights reserved, DACS/Artimage 2023
Image courtesy White Cube
Appliquéd blanket
244 x 193 cm (96.06 x 75.98 in.)

Tilly Du Buisson

Connection

Hannah Hill, a craftivist, emphasises the importance of community in needlework when she says: 'Embroidery is something that gave me a voice, gave me confidence, it connected me with so many people'. Needlework lends itself to community. Women have long gathered in spaces like community centres, the home and now the internet to sew and knit together and whilst doing so have been able to share stories and find solidarity. Not only have women been connected with each other through needlework but it has also allowed them to connect with themselves. During times of hardship and oppression needlework has facilitated such an important space for women to amplify their voices and assert themselves. The nature of needlework encourages a deep personal connection because of the tactile nature of the practice. Practising needlework means using one's body to create art which means women have been able to connect more deeply with themselves and their work. This chapter focuses on how needlework has allowed women to connect with themselves and other women and how this connection has enabled them to gain strength to fight prejudice and gender stereotypes.

In her essay *Sisterhood: Political Solidarity Between Women*, bell hooks writes about creating 'a sustained feminist movement' by learning 'the true meaning and value of sisterhood'. hooks talks about how women are divided by race, class and sexuality because of white supremacist capitalist patriarchy ideology. She writes that 'solidarity strengthens resistance struggle. There can be no mass-based feminist movement to end sexist oppression without a united front - women must take the initiative and demonstrate the power of solidarity'. hooks highlights the importance of solidarity because a movement can be much more effective with varying perspectives and voices. To achieve this 'true meaning' of solidarity and sisterhood, hooks critiques the concept of 'common oppression' which, within the context of feminism, refers to the idea that all women share the same struggles and oppression. However, as hooks points out, that may be oversimplifying the unique and complex experiences different groups of women face. Despite these internal differences in the experiences of oppression, hooks calls for solidarity, focusing on the idea that 'bonding can occur only when these divisions are confronted'. It is key to recognise hooks's emphasis on a diverse community within feminism.

As Simone de Beauvoir points out, women have been punished for their bodies and their bodies have been objectified. However, needlework can allow women to reclaim agency over their body due to the tactility of the practice. Co-founder of Black Girl Knit Club, Sicgmone Kludje highlights the way needlework can offer emotional healing and support in an interview for MyLondon: 'There's something about when you are connecting with your hands that allows your mind to switch off. Knitting is a bridge to discuss our emotions, especially as Black women'. She recognises the importance of needlework's tactile nature within these knitting groups and how it allows women to connect with themselves. This connection to the self can lead to self-empowerment and self-awareness which builds sisterhood.

Needlework has offered women the opportunity to address divisions within feminism by facilitating a space to gather and share their experiences. The 'Protest Banner Lending Library' by artist Aram Han Sifuentes is an example of how needlework can create a diverse community around it. As an immigrant woman of colour, Sifuentes was longing for community after the inauguration of Trump in 2017 which is when she began making her banners of protest. As Sifuntes couldn't protest on the streets due to the risk of deportation, she created this library where those people who could protest would be able to check out her words and take them on to the streets. The banner library and workshops expanded with thousands of banners being made all across America. Sifuentes wrote in an article for Craft Council: 'I sew with disenfranchised people creating a space for subversion, protest and empowerment, enabling people to collectively take a stance, talk back to power and fight for a better world'. Through her banners, Sifuentes creates a space to amplify the voices of marginalised people, ensuring everyone's perspectives are heard. But Sifunentes's impact goes beyond banners: the community she creates uplifts oppressed voices, and thus embodies hooks's 'true meaning of solidarity'.

Not only does needlework allow women to connect with each other today, it also allows them to connect with the women of the past. Indeed, the tactility of the fabric allows for a physical connection across generations with women of the past. By being able to look at and feel pieces of needlework from the past, we can learn about the rich history of women all across the world, further enriching our understanding of women's history. The women of the Chilean arpilleras workshops, to whose work I now turn, demonstrate how women have used the needle to fight oppression and tell stories for the world. Their stories give women today hope and urge us to learn from the past.

During the 1970s, women in Chile transformed the traditional craft of embroidery into a radical tool of resistance with their vibrant patchwork pictures. Dayna Caldwell writes about the brave women of Chile who reclaimed needlework to tell stories, heal and stitch history in 'The Chilean Arpilleristas: Changing National Politics Through Tapestry Work'. Caldwell writes about how, in 1973, General Augusto Pinochet overthrew elected socialist President Salvador Allende, beginning his 17 year long dictatorship where he violated many human rights laws. During this time, women faced many challenges as Pichot enforced a rule that women weren't allowed to work, instead forced to stay at home to perform a domestic role. Men were abducted, tortured and killed to eradicate leftist politics. This traumatised women; they lost their loved ones as well as their financial support, unable to work themselves.

Despite their suffering, women came together to secretly set up workshops, using the practice closest to home to document and resist. They gathered scraps of fabric to tell stories and express their heartache. Caldwell writes that 'driven by their collective memory, the arpilleristas seemingly broke from traditional gender roles by publicly protesting the human rights violations'. She highlights how Chilean women subvert traditional gender stereotypes around needlework and femininity. The workshops encouraged women to share their stories and daily life under occupation, giving us an insight into what it meant to be a woman in Chile at that time.

The arpilleras were sold and shipped abroad by Vicariate of Solidarity, a human rights organisation in Chile during that time. The sales of the arpilleras helped women buy food and support their families as well as helping the world to understand the injustices happening in Chile. These women played such an important role in the fight against the dictatorship; they spoke to the world, calling for help. Caldwell quotes Chilean arpillerist, Violeta Morale who said: 'We not only wanted to embroider and cry out our grief, but we also wished to sing our message of protest'. Chilean women were able to tell stories to the world but they were also able to heal from the trauma of losing their family. Through sewing patches together, they were able to literally and metaphorically piece things back together. The workshops offered women the opportunity to express their feelings and find solidarity with other women going through the same injustice. Figure 9 is an arpilleras by an unknown artist that reads 'never surrender or stray from the path'. This is a clear message of hope; the arpilleras represents the strength and resilience of the women of Chile.

These narratives of hope and resilience from the past serve as inspiration for women today, urging them to advocate for the rights of women all across the world, particularly where war and dictatorships persist. Through needlework, we can have a rich diversity of voices within feminism by understanding the histories of women worldwide. The Chilean arpilleras encourage us to unite in communities through the shared medium of the needle. As the Chilean arpilleras and Sifuentes's banner library shows, the needle can be used to answers hooks's call to uplift marginalised voices and build collective strength. Both the arpilleras and banner library reclaim the needle from its past, transforming it into a weapon of resistance.

[NO TITLE], Unknown female artist, Chile

From Arpilleras: group of 20 patchwork pictures from Chile
Photo: Tate

Conclusion

By learning about the historical ties needlework has with femininity, we've been able to ask whether it is possible to reclaim a historically oppressive practice within an emancipatory feminist project. I have followed the journey of needlework from the 13th to the 20th century, examining how needlework gradually transitioned into a feminine practice. We saw how, during the 13th and 14th centuries, middle and upper-class women were pushed out of the commercial production of needlework, marking the shift towards women being confined to the home. The idea that women must stay in the home and that they were less strong, intellectual beings prevailed into the 16th century. We learned that largely because of the domestic sphere, and the purpose which women's needlework served at the time, the practice was undervalued. This highlights the need for reclamation. The oppression of the needle is evident; women had their education transformed into domestic labour, suffering the weight of patriarchy through needlework.

To answer the question of whether or not women's return to needlework perpetuates or transforms gender norms, I analysed the works of artists like Bourgeois and Emin. We saw how both of these artists challenge traditional ideas of femininity with their unconventional use of needlework. By looking at their work through the perspectives of feminist theorists Butler and Jones, I argued that Bourgeois and Emin have strategically employed essentialism to reclaim needlework from its oppressive past.

Jones's exploration of essentialism within feminist art acknowledges the complex nature of essentialism within feminism because of a deep-rooted essentialism within society. She recognises how it would be hard to completely ignore femininity when addressing feminism and that the transformation of oppressive gender norms may involve apparent, strategic essentialism. Applying Jones's ideas to the work of Bourgeois, we saw how the artist reclaims needlework by blending this traditionally 'feminine' practice with symbols of strength like the spider to create a new image of women. Similarly, we saw how Emin disrupts conventional expectations of femininity by blending pink floral patchworks with vulgar language. Both artists have used needlework like a disguise; they've been able to address uncomfortable topics and challenge gender through this apparently soft and feminine practice.

By drawing parallels between Emin's work and Butler's theory on drag I was able to really discover the power of Emin's work. Just as drag magnifies traits of masculinity and femininity for performance, revealing the performative nature of gender, Emin takes on these symbols with deliberate intensity. Her overt use of gendered imagery, at once delicate and raw, doesn't just mimic traditional ideas of 'masculine' and 'feminine' but reveals their fluidity. Emin's art makes a statement that gender is not innate but a role we slip into, mould and even overturn.

Looking at the use of needlework allows us to see how traditional gender norms can be complicated, using the needle to explore gender in all of its complexity. The use of needles has allowed us to understand the ways that existing traditional ideas can transition into such complex meanings. The rich history of needlework provides an opportunity for women to disrupt those past ideas by transforming the practice today; needlework is the perfect medium for women to express a range of perspectives and stories. Hopefully we can all adopt a more complex understanding of strategic essentialism within feminist art, like Jones's. This will allow feminism to be much more inclusive and diverse by not excluding certain ideas based on their initial appearance.

Both artists' use of strategic essentialism allows us to understand the complexity of feminist art and femininity. We have recognised the diverse range of ways gender can be expressed which allows us to view femininity as a fluid concept. These artists demonstrate how gender norms can be deconstructed, resonating with Butler's ideas around gender fluidity. We can look towards Bourgeois and Emin to broaden our understanding of gender, which will ultimately create a more inclusive and diverse feminist movement. They both represent how the journey ahead for needlework is long and complex. Thanks to these artists, society is beginning to perceive needlework beyond its traditional connotations of femininity and domesticity. This paves the way for more people to get involved and explore the practice to go beyond ridgid binary constructs.

However, despite the progress made in the reclaiming of needlework, we still have a lot of work to do. Many women are still facing oppression because of the practice. In 2013, for example, a tragic disaster of Rana Plaza in Bangladesh occurred where 1,134 mainly female garment workers died due to the collapse of an unsafe garment factory building. We need to consider broader issues, like colonialism and capitalism, to ensure that women all over the world no longer have to suffer because of needlework. We need to draw inspiration from the likes of bell hooks and Sifuentes to uplift marginalised voices. It is crucial we are actively questioning how we can support these women all across the world and how we can advocate for better work conditions, improved pay and challenge our consumerist ways. We can use the subversive power of the needle to stand up from these women and we can be inspired by the many strategies that the women I've discussed in this essay use.

While this essay questions whether women have truly reclaimed needlework, and explores the ways in which they may have done that, it also serves as a celebration of the diverse ways women have used needlework to challenge other forms of oppression such as war. This essay has aimed to acknowledge and honour the women who have paved the way for the exciting future of needlework. The creative journeys of these women offer profound inspiration, encouraging each of us to explore deeply personal narratives through our own art. In my own practice, I turned to needlework as a medium to express my experience and emotions surrounding the role of being a young caregiver. Through combining childhood materials with personal narratives, I began to unearth the complexities

Conclusion

of care, connection and identity woven into this part of my life. Most importantly, it gave me a great opportunity to have conversations that I've never had before. Learning about the connection and community that one can find from needlework remains a great inspiration for us all within the feminist movement. Just like how the Chilean arpilleras were sent all over the world so that everyone could hear their stories, we can find ways to uplift a range of voices in women's needlework exhibitions. Needlework is such a universal practice, and it offers such an opportunity for people to connect across cultures and experiences. I recently came across a video of a Palestinian woman 'working under the bombing' to knit hats for children in her community. This video represents strength and how needlework can offer community and hope in times of hardship. This video of her knitting inspires us all over the world to gather in communities and find pockets of hope to fight for peace around the world. There are many examples of how through needlework we can be inspired to keep advocating for the rights of all people. This essay serves as a reminder of the power of needlework to connect, inspire us and achieve a more diverse understanding of women.

Bibliography

Simone de Beauvoir, (1956) *The Second Sex*. London : Jonathan Cape.

Alter Mark, L. (2020) *Knitting Has Become The Cool Activity During The Coronavirus Crisis*. Available at: www.forbes.com

Kleiman, S. Ezzel, M. Frost, C. (2009) *Reclaiming critical analysis: The social harms of "bitch"*. Available at: www.jmu.edu

Butler, J. (2006) *Gender Trouble*. Routledge Classics. London, England: Routledge.

Navneet Kaur, S. *Profanity and women - a linguistic analysis of language ...* Available at: www.diva-portal.org

Jones, A. (2019) *Essentialism, feminism, and art: spaces where woman 'Oozes Away'*. In: Robinson, H; Buszek, M E (ed.). *Companion to feminist art and theory*. Oxford: Blackwell.

Vinebaum, L. (2020) *The Subversive Stitch Revisited*. In: Harris, J (ed.). *A Companion to Textile Culture*. Oxford: Blackwell.

Parkinson, H. (2023) *Marina Abramović has broken a 255-year-old glass ceiling. why did it take so long?*. The Guardian. Available at: www. theguardian.com

Polonsky, N. (2019) *Female artists are finally in our galleries – let's keep them there*. The Guardian. Available at: www.the guardian.com

Vinebaum, L. (2021) *Unsettling 'women's work'*. Available at: img-cache.oppcdn.com

Mark, J.J. (2024) *Women in the Middle Ages, World History Encyclopedia*. Available at: www.worldhistory.org

King-Hammond, L. (2022) *Harriet Powers, AWARE Women artists / Femmes artistes*. Available at: awarewomenartists.com

Ferrier, M. (2016) *Louise Bourgeois – the reluctant hero of feminist art, The Guardian*. Available at: www.theguardian.com

Souter, A. (2018) *Louise Bourgeois: Subversive Stitching, Roman Road Journal*. Available at: romanroadjournal.com

Bibliography

Acosta, M. Mistry, T. Varga, S. (2022) *Why are Women not so Successful as Men in the Professional Kitchen? Journal of Hospitality & Tourism Cases*, Available at: doi.org

Steavenson, W. (2022) *How things are changing for women in the kitchen*. Available at: www.ft.com

Copley, M. (2019) *First threads: Preparing girls for life? - british-schoolsmuseum.org.uk, First Threads: preparing girls for life?* Available at: britishschoolsmuseum.org.uk

Bashir, I. (2022) *How quilts became a canvas for black American artists to preserve history*. Available at: www.sleep.com

Schippers, M, Sapp, E. G. (2012). *Reading Pulp Fiction: Femininity and power in second and third wave feminist theory* Available at: doi.org

Letts, Q. (2014) *Tracey Emin's vulgar show proves the art luvvies are dragging civilisation backwards: Quentin Letts finds the artist's latest exhibition both embarrassing and infuriating*. Daily Mail Online. Available at: www.dailymail.co.uk

Gipson, F. (2022) *Women's Work: From feminine arts to feminist art*. Quarto Publishing.

Barzey, W. (2022) *There was no-one who looked like us at our local Knitting Club*. My London. Available at: www.mylondon.news

Sifuentes, A.H. (2020) *Protest making: How crafting collectively can empower disenfranchised people, Protest making: how crafting collectively can empower disenfranchised people*. Available at: www.craftscouncil.org.uk

hooks, b (1986) *Sisterhood: Political Solidarity between Women*. Feminist Review. Available at: doi.org

Caldwell, L. D, (2012) *The Chilean Arpilleristas: Changing National Politics Through Tapestry Work*. Textile Society of America Symposium Proceedings. Available at: digitalcommons.unl.edu

Textile Society of America Symposium Proceedings. Available at: digitalcommons.unl.edu

Muñoz, S.F. (2020) *Arpilleras the Vessels of Chile's Resistance*. Textile Society of America. Available at: digitalcommons.unl.edu

Coxon, A., Fer, B. and Müller-Schareck, M. (2018) *Anni Albers*. New Haven: Yale University Press.

Actionaid (2019) *Six years on from Bangladesh's Rana Plaza Tragedy, one in five survivors' health is deteriorating*. ActionAid International. Available at: actionaid.org

Needlework

© 2025 Tilly Du Buisson, www.tillydubuisson.com

Edited by: Paul Baxter
Copy Editor: Jessie Jones
Graphic Design: Marco Ugolini, www.objectif.co.uk
Published by: Rova Editions Limited

ISBN 978-10-369035-5-8

Worldwide distribution:
Public Knowledge Books Limited
sales@publicknowledgebooks.com

Printed by Drukmania, PL